ALL IN ONE:

66 Pulled Pork Recipes – Juicy, Tender and Dangerously Delicious

Icons from Freepik from flaticon.com
Iconnice from flaticon.com and GoodWare from flaticon.com

Images from Brent Hofacker/Shutterstock.com, Elena Veselova/Shutterstock.com, Alexander Raths/Shutterstock.com, Dar1930/Shutterstock.com, from my point of view/Shutterstock.com, stockcreations/Shutterstock.com, Olga Militsova/Shutterstock.com, VICUSCHKA/Shutterstock.com, jenwong/Shutterstock.com

Table of Contents

INTRODUCTION

Everybody loves pulled pork! The long-time staple of Southern BBQ has blown up in recent years, with restaurants and homes all over the world serving up their takes on the beloved dish. Simple, savory and oh-so versatile - what's not to love?

For some, however, the prospect of slow-cooking or barbecuing their own pulled pork feast can seem daunting. The internet is teeming with tips, tricks and go-to methods for rustling up some succulent pork, but finding the right method for you can be a dizzying experience. Should you roast low and slow in an oven overnight or invest in a slow cooker? What's the difference between a rub and a marinade? What cuts of meat should you use and where can you buy them? And is pulled pork only suitable for BBQs?

In this book I'll cover all the basics of making a truly show-stopping pulled pork dish:

How to utilize the kitchen equipment you already own to cook perfectly tender meat, whether you have a crockpot, a smoker or just a standard kitchen oven.

I'll walk you through which cuts of meat work best, resulting in maximum flavor and perfect texture every time.

Clueless about rubs and marinades? Check out my cheat sheet for some simple, time-saving kitchen hacks and learn to utilize spices like a pro. It couldn't be easier!

Best of all, I'll show you that pulled pork doesn't just belong at the BBQ. With my extensive range of recipes, including 20 sides and small plates, 20 appetizers and 20 entrees, you'll learn that pulled pork can be the perfect ingredient of a variety of dishes spanning multiple cuisines.

Whether you're looking to feed a party or just yourself, this book has a recipe for you.

So, what are you waiting for? Let's get cooking!

Equipment and Kitchen Staples

Before we get started on choosing the best cooking method for your meat, there's a couple of things you'll need to make your meal prep as stress-free and easy as possible.

Make sure you have aluminum foil or Saran Wrap and sufficient space in your refrigerator. This is absolutely essential when marinating your meat, whether it's for a few hours or overnight.

Give yourself a clear, wide working space. You're going to be mixing sauces, preparing rubs and tearing up some tender pork - make sure you give yourself enough room to complete each task, without the fear of tipping something over or spilling essential ingredients.

You may have already seen BBQ "claws" online or at the store. These nifty gadgets are like spiked knuckle-dusters, designed to make shredding meat quick and easy. If you don't have your own set of claws, don't worry about it. As long as you have two strong, sturdy forks you'll be able to achieve the same effect.

Once you've got your kitchen in top shape, let's move on to the fun part!

THE  BASICS

CHOOSING YOUR MEAT

One of the questions I get asked the most is, "What cut of meat should I use for pulled pork?"

Most of us are probably familiar with chops or pork loin, but neither of those seem suitable for a delicious BBQ feast. So what cut works best and where can you get it?

Typically, when making pulled pork, you'll want to use a pork shoulder. Fair warning - this is a big piece of meat. Pork shoulders can weigh as much as 18 lbs., and will comfortably feed over twenty people.

If you're not feeding an army, however, you'll probably want to stick to a Boston Butt. This is the top cut of the shoulder and can weigh anywhere from 5 to 10 lbs. It's a nicely marbled cut of meat, meaning it's extra flavorful. Usually you can buy it with or without a bone. Though it won't make a huge difference when it comes to cooking, having a bone-in does add more flavor. This beauty will feed a crowd of 12 or more people. When making pulled pork, prepare to have a lot of tasty leftovers that can be utilized in countless amazing dishes (more on that later).

Alternatively, you can get a Picnic Shoulder, which is the lower end of a pork shoulder. This has a larger bone than the Boston Butt, which you'll have to cut around when pulling your pork. It also has less fat marbling and more connective tissue than a Boston Butt, so cooking low and slow is absolutely essential. Luckily for us, low and slow is the name of the game when making pulled pork!

Finding these cuts in your run-of-the-mill supermarket can sometimes be tricky. But don't worry, this can be a blessing in disguise. Broadly speaking, supermarket meats will have less flavor than what you can buy in a butcher shop, mostly because of the industrial way the meat is reared for grocery stores.

An experienced butcher will also be able to help you choose the best cut and weight for your meal. So you'll get a better quality meat and some expert advice if you go to a local butcher.

SMOKER, CROCKPOT OR OVEN?

So you've got your meat - now what?

There's more than one way to make perfect pulled pork, so it's just a matter of finding the method that suits you and your equipment.

Chances are if you Google "How to make pulled pork", you'll find a lot of columns and articles by BBQ aficionados singing the praises of their smokers. Smokers are designed to maintain a low temperature (usually around 225 degrees F) while slow-cooking meat with the aid of smoke. There's a variety of different kinds of smokers, ranging from small backyard affairs to smokers big enough to cook a full hog.

The benefits of using a smoker over other methods of cooking are pretty straight-forward: You get tender, slow-cooked meat infused with a delicious smoky flavor. When cooking pork in your smoker, it's best to stick with hickory or maple wood chips. Though oak is a standard go-to for smoking meats, hickory and maple will add subtle complimentary flavors to your meat. Soak your wood chips in water overnight to stop them from burning up in the smoker and add a fresh handful of chips every 30 minutes while cooking. Be sure to spritz your meat each time you add more chips to keep it moist and tender. A quick spritz of apple juice will do the trick and bring out the sweet natural flavors of the meat.

Before cooking your meat, let it sit for 30-45 minutes at room temperature. If you place it on the grill straight from the fridge, it will be too cold and the outside will burn. Placed on the grill at room temperature, it should cook nicely and evenly.

Once your meat is ready, place it on your smoker with the layer of fat facing down. Allow to cook for about two hours before flipping over. Keeping your smoker's temperature between 225 - 250 F, allow 90 minutes cooking time per pound of meat. So if you're cooking a 10 lb. Boston Butt, you're looking at 15 hours of cooking. Good things come to those who wait!

Wrap the pork in foil for the final two hours and keep it in the smoker. Cook until your meat thermometer reads 195 - this means the fat has been rendered, leaving nothing but melt-in-your-mouth, tender meat.

Now, not all of us have access to a smoker or 15 hours to spend cooking. But that doesn't mean you can't still enjoy some delicious pulled pork! Crockpots and standard ovens can save a lot of time and will still result in a beautiful bit of meat.

When cooking with a Crockpot or other slow cooker, place your cut in the cooker with the rest of your ingredients (we'll get to those shortly. Set your cooker on low and leave to cook for 8 hours. Alternatively, you can set it to high and cook for 4 hours. These times are based on a 5 lb. cut, as anything bigger isn't likely to fit in your slow-cooker. The outcome will basically be the same - succulent meat that falls right off the bone!

Cooking times in a standard oven are similarly speedy. Season your meat and roast it at 450 degrees F for an hour. After the first hour, reduce your heat to about 300 degrees and place your pork in a deep roasting dish or dutch oven. Pour in your vegetables, stock, and sauces and cover with a lid or tightly-wrapped foil for another 3-4 hours.

While slow-cooker and oven pork has to be smaller for practical purposes, you don't have to sacrifice intensely delicious flavor. Even if you're not using a smoker, you can still get that trademark BBQ taste by adding a few drops of liquid smoke into your mix or a couple of teaspoons of smoked paprika. Speaking of which, let's talk seasonings....

SEASONINGS, MARINADES AND TIPS

One of the greatest things about cooking pork is all the creative ways you can season it. It's such a versatile meat, pairing beautifully with spicy, savory flavors as well as sweet, fruity ones. Here are just some of my favorite ways to prepare pork, resulting in a dish loaded with exciting flavors.

Before you season your meat, I'd advise trimming the layer of fat until it's about 1/8th of an inch thick. This will allow your seasonings to better penetrate the flesh, while still keeping the meat juicy and tender.

RUBS

If you're cooking your pork in a smoker, you'll probably want to give it a nice ol' rub beforehand. Rubs are mixes of spices and herbs that you massage into the meat and allow to chill before cooking.

Your classic rub should be a balance of sweet and spicy.

Try using two tablespoons of brown sugar, two tablespoons of salt, ¼ cup of chili powder, ¼ cup of paprika and ¼ cup of garlic powder. Massage the mixture into your meat thoroughly before wrapping tightly in saran wrap and keeping in your fridge overnight.

The brown sugar will give a rich, caramelized sweetness to the meat, while the spices will bring out the pork's natural savory flavors. This rub will give you a standard, traditional BBQ taste that will compliment most of the dishes in this book.

There are a variety of different rubs out there, so don't be afraid to play around. If you're a fan of garlic, why not try swapping out garlic powder for finely minced fresh garlic? Like your food a bit hotter? Add mustard powder or cayenne pepper to your rub. Once you've mastered my basic rub, see where your creativity will take you!

MARINADES AND BASES

Though you'll also be using a rub if you're cooking with a slow-cooker or oven, the bulk of your flavor is going to come from what you put into the dish with your pork.

For this, you not only have to pay attention to flavor, but also moisture. For crockpot dishes, line the bottom of your crockpot with half a white onion, diced. Place your pork on top, then add a cup of vegetable stock, ¼ cup of tomato paste, a ¼ cup of apple cider vinegar and 8 oz. of BBQ sauce.

For cooking in the oven, the method is pretty similar. Roast your pre-rubbed pork for an hour, then place in a deep roasting dish or dutch oven lined with half a white onion, diced. Add the other ingredients, cover with a lid or tightly wrapped foil and cook.

Another good base for dishes like these is to use 1 cup of apple juice instead of the vegetable stock. You can also substitute the BBQ sauce with 1.5 cups of ketchup, 2 tablespoons of brown sugar and 2 tablespoons of Worcestershire sauce. Try them out and see which method you prefer!

Don't forget, if you want to recreate the hickory flavors of smoked BBQ pork, add 2 tablespoons of smoked paprika or a few drops of liquid smoke. This will give you an authentic smoky flavor, with none of the fuss!

BRINING

Another popular question I get from aspiring BBQ-ers is whether or not they should brine their pork before cooking.

Brining involves soaking your meat in a mixture of salt, water and sometimes other ingredients for anywhere from 12-24 hours before cooking. While there are certainly benefits to brining, it's not essential.

Brining can help keep your meat moist while cooking, but if you're cooking using a slow-cooker or oven this shouldn't be an issue anyway. It can also further infuse your meat with flavor, especially if you choose to add apple juice and/or maple syrup to your salt water mixture.

If you're curious and have time to spare, I'd recommend mixing 3 cups of water with ¼ cup of salt and allowing your meat to soak for 24 hours. A Boston Butt won't require brining, thanks to its good marbling. But if you choose to cook a Picnic Shoulder, brining might help break down that connective tissue more, resulting in a more tender end product.

Now that we've covered the basics, let's put your new knowledge to the test with some mouth-watering recipes!

SNACKS, SIDES AND SMALL PLATES

Loaded pulled pork potato skins

 1 hr 15 mins

6 - 8 servings

Ingredients:

4 russet potatoes

2 cups pulled pork

½ cup shredded sharp cheddar

½ cup shredded mozzarella cheese

2 tbsp melted butter

1 tbsp oil

For the sauce:

1 ½ cups ketchup

½ cup water

½ cup apple cider vinegar

½ cup brown sugar

¼ cup mustard powder

2 tsp paprika

2 tsp garlic powder

1 tsp salt

1 tsp ground black pepper

Garnishes: sour cream, crispy bacon, green onion, hot sauce

Instructions:

1. Preheat your oven to 400 degrees. Wash and dry your potatoes and rub oil into the skins. Pierce the skins with a fork and put them on a lined baking tray in the oven. Allow to cook for one hour.

2. While waiting on your potatoes to cook, mix your bbq sauce. This will prevent the meat from drying out later. This recipe should yield about 3 cups of bbq sauce.

3. Once you've mixed all your sauce ingredients, add the pork and allow to simmer in a pot for 30 minutes.

4. When your potatoes are soft, take them out of the oven and slice them in half lengthwise. Scoop out the soft insides of the potatoes, making sure to keep at least ¼ inch of flesh inside the skins.

5. Brush the inside and outside of your potato skins with your melted butter, then load with your pulled pork.

6. Sprinkle equal parts mozzarella and cheddar cheese on your potato skins. Lower your oven temperature to 350 and bake until the cheese has melted.

7. Garnish and serve.

Bbq pulled pork sliders

 2 hrs 30 mins

 8 servings

Ingredients:

3 - 4 cups pulled pork

1 - 2 cups bbq sauce

For the buns:

3 cups bread flour

1 cup warm water

3 tbsp warm milk

3 tbsp softened unsalted butter

2 tsp sugar

2 tsp salt

2 tsp dried yeast

2 eggs

Instructions:

1. Using the same bbq sauce recipe as before, mix your sauce and pork, and put to one side.

2. Mix your water, milk, sugar and yeast in a bowl. Leave for about 5 minutes or until it starts to foam.

3. Pour your flour into a mixing bowl, and mix with the salt and butter. Mix with your hands or a spatula until the mixture resembles breadcrumbs.

4. Beat one egg, then add to the flour mixture along with the foamy yeast, water, milk and sugar.

5. Use your hands and knead until the mixture reaches a thick, consistent state.

6. Roll into a ball, and cover with a damp cloth. Allow to rise for 1 - 2 hours.

7. Preheat your oven to 400 degrees.

8. Once your dough has doubled in size, separate into 8 small circles and place on a paper-lined baking tray.

9. Place a tray filled with 1 cup of water at the bottom of your oven. Doing this will release steam, keeping your buns moist while baking.

10. Beat your remaining egg and brush each bun with an egg wash.

11. Place your buns in the oven and allow to bake for 15 - 20 minutes or until golden.

12. While your buns bake, simmer your pork and bbq sauce mixture on the stove.

13. When your buns are fully baked, allow to stand on a wire rack to cool.

14. Slice your buns and fill with your bbq pork and additional fillings of your choice.

Sweet and savory pulled pork quesadilla

20 - 30 mins

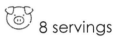8 servings

Ingredients:

2.5 cups pulled pork

2 large flour tortillas

2 cups shredded pepper jack cheese

1 red bell pepper

1 green bell pepper

1 tbsp olive oil

For the salsa:

3 large, fresh tomatoes, diced

1 clove minced garlic

½ red onion, diced

1 whole jalapeno pepper, minced

Juice of ½ a lime

½ cup chopped cilantro

2 tsp sugar

1 tbsp apple cider vinegar

¼ tsp salt

¼ tsp cumin

Instructions:

1. Prepare your salsa ingredients and mix in a bowl, or pulse in a food processor until it reaches your desired consistency.

2. Lay out one of your tortillas and generously spread a layer of salsa on top.

3. Top with your pork, sliced bell peppers and sprinkle with cheese.

4. Place the second tortilla on top and brush with olive oil.

5. Lightly oil a skillet or large frying pan and fry the quesadilla for 3-4 minutes each side, or until the cheese melts and the tortillas become crisp.

6. Cut into 8 equal slices and serve.

Fiery pulled pork nachos

 30 mins

 8 - 10 servings

Ingredients:

1 8 - 10 oz bag of tortilla chips

2 cups pulled pork

½ cup shredded cheddar cheese

½ cup shredded pepper jack cheese

½ cup sliced jalapeno peppers

½ red onion, thinly sliced

2 large tomatoes, diced

½ cup black beans

½ cup sour cream

Garnish: chopped cilantro, hot sauce of your choice

Instructions:

1. Preheat your oven to 400 degrees.

2. Line a baking tray with paper, and empty out your tortilla chips. Make sure to spread them as evenly as you can.

3. Spread your pork on top of the chips, and cover with your diced tomatoes and black beans.

4. Sprinkle the cheddar and pepper jack cheeses, then add your jalapenos and sliced onion.

5. Place in the oven and cook until cheese is melted and bubbling.

6. Remove from the oven and allow to cool for 3 - 5 minutes.

7. Generously spoon your sour cream on top, and finish with cilantro and hot sauce.

Pulled pork spring rolls

1 hr

6 - 8 servings

Ingredients:

2.5 cups pulled pork

12 - 16 rice paper wraps

1 cup bean sprouts

1 carrot, grated

½ white cabbage, grated

1 inch ginger, grated

1 tbsp soy sauce

1 tsp fish sauce

¼ bunch cilantro, chopped

½ cup sesame oil, for frying.

Instructions:

- Fill a bowl with hot, but not boiling, water. Place your rice paper wraps in the water one at a time until they are soft and pliable.

- Mix your pork with the ginger, soy sauce and fish sauce.

- Lay your wrap flat, and spoon your seasoned pork in a thin line on the far side of the wrap. Be careful not to add too much or the wrap will tear when you try to roll it later.

- Lay the thin strips of carrot and cabbage, along with the bean sprouts, on top of the pork.

- Sprinkle with cilantro.

- Fold the top and bottom of your wrap inwards, and roll tightly from left to right. Imagine you're rolling a tiny burrito.

- Heat your oil in a frying pan until it sizzles when anything is added.

- Fry your rolls in small batches to ensure even cooking.

- Fry for 5 minutes each or until the rice paper is crisp and golden.

- Remove from pan and dab with kitchen paper to remove excess oil.

- Serve with sweet chilidipping sauce or sriracha.

Crispy pulled pork taquitos

 30 mins

 12 servings

Ingredients:

2.5 cups of pulled pork

12 corn tortillas

1.5 cups of salsa

1.5 cups shredded queso

½ cup vegetable oil, for frying

Garnish: sour cream, guacamole

Instructions:

1. Mix your pork, salsa and queso in a bowl. You can use the same salsa recipe from this book's sweet and savory pulled pork quesadilla recipe.

2. Using a microwave or an oven, warm your tortillas for 1 minute. This will soften them and make them easier to roll.

3. Spoon your filling mixture into your tortillas. Wrap and secure with a toothpick.

4. Heat your oil in a frying pan until sizzling. Fry your taquitos in batches of 3.

5. Fry for 2 minutes, or until golden brown. Be sure to rotate your taquitos so they cook evenly.

6. Remove from pan and rest on kitchen paper to remove excess oil.

7. Serve with sour cream, guacamole, or the dip of your choice.

Taco pork stuffed peppers

 1 hr

 6 servings

Ingredients:

3 cups pulled pork

6 orange or yellow bell peppers

1 cup black beans

½ cup water

½ yellow onion, diced

1 clove of garlic, minced

¼ cup olive oil

2 tsp cumin

2 tsp chili powder

1 tsp smoked paprika

1 cup shredded cheddar

½ tsp salt

½ tsp ground black pepper

Instructions:

1. Heat a tablespoon of oil in a frying pan before adding the onion and garlic. Fry until both are soft and golden.

2. Add pork, black beans, water and spices. Turn heat down to a simmer and stir occasionally.

3. Cut the tops off your bell peppers and remove seeds.

4. Preheat your oven to 375 degrees and line a baking tray with paper.

5. Place your peppers on the baking tray. Drizzle with oil and season with salt and pepper.

6. Once the moisture in your pork and bean mixture has reduced by half, remove from the stove and spoon the mixture into the peppers.

7. Sprinkle with cheese and put in the oven for 20 - 30 minutes or until the peppers are soft with lightly-browned edges.

8. Serve with salsa or guacamole.

Hoisin pork pancakes

 45 mins

 12 servings

Ingredients:

2.5 cups pulled pork

1 carrot, julienned

1 cucumber, julienned

4 green onions, thinly sliced vertically

For the pancakes:

2 cups flour

1 cup boiling water

½ tsp salt

2 tbsp sesame oil

For the sauce:

4 tbsp soy sauce

2 tbsp smooth, natural peanut butter

2 tbsp water

1 tbsp honey

1 tbsp rice vinegar

1 tbsp sesame oil

1 tsp chinese five spice

1 clove of garlic, minced

1 tsp sriracha (optional)

Instructions:

1. Mix the ingredients for your hoisin sauce until smooth. Seal well and chill in the fridge until needed.

2. Put your flour and salt in a bowl, gradually stirring in the boiling water.

3. Allow to cool. When dough is too hot, it can be very difficult to knead.

4. Once your dough has cooled, knead until smooth. Cover your bowl and leave the dough to rest for 20 minutes.

5. Heat your sesame oil in a frying pan, and divide your dough into 12 balls.

6. Roll the balls using a rolling pin until they are thin and delicate pancakes.

7. Fry the pancakes one at a time for 30 seconds each side.

8. Serve with pulled pork, vegetables and hoisin sauce. Load the pancakes as desired.

Spicy pork lettuce roll-ups

 30 mins

 8 servings

Ingredients:

4 cups pulled pork

1 head of romaine lettuce

1.5 cups shredded carrot

1 cup shredded cheddar

For the buffalo sauce:

½ cup melted butter

½ cup hot sauce of your choice

2 tbsp white vinegar

1 tbsp worcestershire sauce

½ tsp garlic powder

Instructions:

- Combine your sauce ingredients and simmer over a low heat. Cook for 1 minute, or until the sauce thickens.

- Mix the sauce with your pork and allow to sit.

- Chop the end off your head of lettuce and separate the leaves. Once separated, wash each leaf and dry with kitchen paper.

- Spoon the buffalo pork into the lettuce leaves and top with carrots and cheese.

- Serve on a platter and roll roughly to eat.

Pork and apple 'slaw

⏱ 30 mins

🐷 6 - 8 servings

Ingredients:

2 cups of pulled pork

2 granny smith apples, grated

1 red cabbage, shredded

1 carrot, grated

½ cup mayonnaise

2 tbsp apple cider vinegar

2 tbsp honey

1 tsp salt

1 tsp ground black pepper

½ lime, juiced

Instructions:

- Mix the mayonnaise, vinegar, honey, lime juice and salt and pepper in a bowl to create the dressing.

- Add the pork, cabbage, apple and carrot. Mix well, allowing for an even coating of dressing.

- Serve right away or allow to sit overnight for greater flavor intensity.

Pulled pork crack slaw

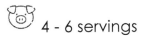 30 mins

4 - 6 servings

Ingredients:

1 cup pulled pork

1 white cabbage, shredded

1 carrot, grated

4 green onions, thinly sliced

2 cloves garlic, minced

1 inch fresh ginger, minced

¼ cup soy sauce

2 tbsp sesame oil

½ tbsp sriracha

1 tsp white vinegar

½ tsp sugar

Garnish: sesame seeds, sriracha sauce

Instructions:

1. Heat your sesame oil in a pan or wok.

2. Add your garlic, ginger and green onions and fry until soft.

3. Add the pork, cabbage and carrot, along with your soy sauce, sriracha, white vinegar and sugar. Stir-fry for 3 - 5 minutes.

4. Remove from heat and empty into a bowl. Leave to cool for 15 - 20 minutes.

5. Serve immediately or chill overnight for greater flavor intensity. Sprinkle with sesame seeds and/or drizzle with sriracha as a garnish.

Loaded bbq sweet potato fries

 40 mins

 4 servings

Ingredients:

2 cups pulled pork

4 large sweet potatoes

½ cup bbq sauce

½ cup cheddar cheese

½ red onion, thinly sliced

1 avocado, sliced

2 green onions

2 tbsp olive oil

1 tsp paprika

1 tsp garlic powder

½ tsp salt

½ tsp ground black pepper

Instructions:

1. Peel your sweet potatoes and slice them into ½ inch strips.

2. Preheat your oven to 400 degrees and oil a baking tray.

3. Empty your fries into the tray and sprinkle with salt, pepper, paprika and garlic powder. Shake thoroughly to ensure every fry is well-seasoned.

4. Place the fries in the oven and cook for 15 - 20 minutes or until they are soft.

5. Mix your pork with your bbq sauce. I recommend trying my bbq sauce recipe from my potato skins recipe at the beginning of this book.

6. Remove fries from the oven and top with pork, cheese and onions. Return to the oven for a further 5 minutes or until the cheese has melted.

7. Remove and top with sliced avocado and green onions. Serve and enjoy!

Bite-size bbq biscuits

 45 mins

20 servings

Ingredients:

3 - 4 cups pulled pork

1 cup bbq sauce

For the biscuits:

2 cups self-rising flour

¾ cup buttermilk

1 stick butter, cubed and softened

2 tsp baking powder

Instructions:

- Preheat your oven to 450 degrees.

- Sift your flour into a bowl and mix with the butter, baking powder and a pinch of salt.

- Mix until the consistency resembles breadcrumbs.

- Form a well in the middle of your mixture and slowly add your buttermilk, mixing until it creates a thick dough.

- Sprinkle your workspace with flour and roll out your dough until about ½ inch thick.

- Cut the dough into 20 circles using a circle cutter.

- Place your biscuits in a baking tray which has been oiled with butter or lard. Place in the oven and allow to bake for 10 minutes or until golden brown.

- While they bake, add the bbq sauce to your pork. I recommend trying my bbq sauce recipe from my potato skins recipe at the beginning of this book.

- Remove biscuits from the oven and allow to cool on a wire rack.

- Once cool, slice your biscuits down the middle and sandwich your pork inside.

- Try adding other fillings like coleslaw or cheddar cheese for fun flavor combinations.

Pork-filled party empanadas

 1 hr 40 mins

 25 - 30 servings

Ingredients:

2 cups pulled pork

1 ½ cups flour

½ cup cream cheese

½ cup butter, softened

1 egg, beaten

½ cup bbq sauce

Instructions:

1. Mix your butter and cream cheese together in a bowl until completely blended.

2. Sift your flower into the butter and cheese mixture and mix well. Form the dough into a ball.

48

3. Cover your dough and chill in the fridge for minimum 1 hour.

4. Mix your pork and bbq sauce. I recommend trying my bbq sauce recipe from my potato skins recipe at the beginning of this book.

5. Preheat your oven to 400 degrees.

6. Remove your dough from the fridge.

7. Sprinkle your workspace with flour and roll out your dough until it is ¼ inch thick.

8. Cut into 25 - 30 circles.

9. Spoon your pork mixture into the middle of each circle. Wash the edges of the dough with your beaten egg and fold.

10. Use a fork to press the edges of the dough together and ensure they won't open while baking.

11. Place your empanadas on a paper-lined baking tray, and wash each of them with your remaining egg.

12. Bake for 20 minutes or until golden brown.

13. Remove from the oven and allow to cool on a wire rack.

14. Serve with the dip of your choice!

Pulled pork and salsa bruschetta

 20 mins

 10 - 12 servings

Ingredients:

2 cups pulled pork

2 cups salsa

1 red onion, sliced

¼ cup sour cream

1 baguette, sliced into 10 -12 pieces

2 tbsp olive oil

1 clove garlic, minced

Instructions:

- Mix your minced garlic with your olive oil.

- Brush each slice of your baguette with the garlic oil, and toast under a broiler or grill until golden.

- Remove once toasted, and top with thinly sliced red onion.

- Spoon your pulled pork on top of the onion, followed by your salsa. I recommend using my salsa recipe from the quesadilla recipe earlier in this book.

- Drizzle with sour cream or dollop lightly.

- Serve and enjoy!

Party size pork pizza puffs

 1 hr 15 mins

8 - 10 servings

Ingredients:

3 cups pulled pork

1.5 cups bbq sauce or marinara sauce

2 cups mozzarella cheese, shredded

1 egg, beaten

For the puff pastry:

2 cups flour

1 stick of butter

¾ cup ice water

½ tsp salt

Instructions:

1. Sift your flour into a bowl and mix with the salt.

2. Break your butter into small, rough chunks and mix with the flour using your hands. Make sure each piece of butter is coated.

3. Gradually add the ice water until the dough sticks together.

4. Cover and chill in the fridge for 20 - 30 mins.

5. Sprinkle your workspace with flour and roll out your dough into a rectangle measuring about 8" x 13".

6. Fold the shorter side towards you and roll out again. Repeat twice more.

7. Cover tightly with saran wrap and chill for another 20 minutes.

8. Roll out once more until about ¼ inch thick.

9. Slice dough into small rectangles and spoon bbq sauce or marinara sauce onto the dough, spreading evenly.

10. Place your pork on one side of the rectangle and sprinkle with cheese.

11. Fold over the other side of the rectangle and close the pocket by pressing the edges with a fork.

12. Wash the pocket with your beaten egg.

13. Place the pockets on a greased baking tray, and put in a preheated oven set to 350 degrees.

14. Bake for 20 minutes or until golden brown.

Pork hash cups

 50 mins

 6 servings

Ingredients:

2 cups pulled pork

2 russet potatoes, peeled and shredded

½ white onion, shredded

2 tbsp flour

1 egg

1 tsp salt

1 tsp ground black pepper

1 cup cheddar cheese, shredded

¼ cup olive oil or melted butter

Instructions:

1. Squeeze as much moisture as you can from the shredded potatoes, before adding them into a bowl with the flour, onion, egg, salt and pepper.

2. Mix well until all lumps of flour are gone and the vegetables are well-coated.

3. Preheat oven to 350 degrees and grease a muffin tray with your oil or butter.

4. Line each cup in the muffin tray with your hash brown mixture.

5. Bake in the oven for 20 - 30 minutes or until the hash brown cups begin to brown.

6. Remove from oven and fill each cup with pulled pork. Sprinkle with cheese.

7. Place back in the oven for another 5 minutes or until the cheese has melted.

8. Remove from oven and allow to cool for up to 5 minutes.

9. Serve with your choice of dip or sauce.

Mini pork quiches

 1 hr 15 mins

 6 servings

Ingredients:

2 cups pulled pork

6 eggs, beaten

2 cups spinach

1 cup swiss cheese, shredded

½ cup cream

½ white onion, thinly sliced

1 tbsp olive oil

1 tsp garlic powder

½ tsp salt

½ tsp ground black pepper

For the shortcrust pastry:

2 cups flour

4 oz butter, diced

4 tbsp ice water

½ tbsp salt

Instructions:

- Combine the flour and salt in a mixing bowl.

- Add the butter and mix with your fingers until it reaches a consistency that resembles breadcrumbs. Be sure to work quickly, so the mixture does not become too warm.

- Gradually add the ice water and mix with a cold knife until the dough sticks together.

- Cover and chill in the fridge for 30 minutes.

- Heat your oil in a pan and fry your onion and spinach until soft. Add your pork and fry for 1-2 minutes before removing from heat. Allow to cool.

- Once cooled, mix your pork, onions and spinach with the eggs, cream, cheese and seasoning. Mix well.

- Sprinkle your workspace with flour and roll out your dough until it is ⅛ inch thick. Cut into 6 circles using a circle cutter.

- Grease a muffin tray with butter and place your circles of dough into the muffin cups.

- Pour your pork and egg mixture evenly into each up.

- Bake in a preheated oven set to 375 degrees for 15 - 20 minutes or until the pastry is firm and golden.

- Allow to cool for up to 5 minutes before removing from the muffin tray.

Buffalo pork tear and share bread

 2 hrs

 6 servings

Ingredients:

1 cup pulled pork

½ cup buffalo sauce

1 cup mozzarella cheese

3 green onions, chopped

For the bread:

3 cups bread flour

1 packet of dry yeast

2 tbsp olive oil

1 cup warm water

1 tsp salt

Instructions:

1. Pour your yeast into your cup of warm water and leave for 5 minutes or until foamy.

2. Sift your flour into a bowl and add the oil and salt.

3. Gradually add the yeast mixture and mix until it forms a sticky dough.

4. Sprinkle flour on your workspace and tip out your dough. Knead until smooth.

5. Return your dough to the bowl and allow to sit in a cool, dry area for 1 hour or until it has doubled in size.

6. Mix your pork with the buffalo sauce. I recommend using the buffalo sauce recipe from my spicy pork lettuce roll-ups earlier in this book.

7. When your dough is ready, again sprinkle flour on your work area and begin to roll out your dough. Roll until the dough is ¼ inch thick.

8. Cut the dough three times across and three times down. This should leave you with 16 rectangles of equal size.

9. Layer your buffalo pork, cheese and green onions on each rectangle.

10. Grease a bread tin. Hold the tin at a 90 degree angle to your countertop.

11. Add your sheets of dough, one at a time, layering them until the tin is full.

12. Sprinkle any additional cheese and onions on top.

13. Put into a preheated oven at 400 degrees, and bake for 30 - 40 minutes or until the bread is brown.

14. Remove from oven and allow to cool on a wire rack.

15. Remove from bread tin - tear, share and enjoy!

Cheesy pulled pork dip

 30 mins

 10 servings

Ingredients:

1 cup pulled pork

1 cup pepper jack cheese

1 cup cheddar cheese

⅓ cup sour cream

2 green onions, chopped

1 tbsp tabasco

1 tsp garlic powder

1 tsp salt

1 tsp ground black pepper

Instructions:

1. Mix your cheeses and sour cream well. Keep at least ¼ cup of both   cheeses.

2. Add in the pork and green onions, and mix thoroughly until well-coated.

3. Add your seasonings and tabasco. Mix.

4. Empty your dip into a skillet or casserole dish.

5. Preheat your oven to 350 degrees.

6. Sprinkle the dip with the remaining cheese and bake in the oven for 15-20 minutes.

7. Remove from the oven and serve with tortillas.

APPETIZERS

Pork and apple salad

 30 mins

 4 servings

Ingredients:

1 cup pulled pork

2 gala apples, cored and sliced

2 sticks celery, chopped

2 romaine lettuces, shredded

½ cup sugar snap peas

For the dressing:

2 tbsp apple cider vinegar

1 tbsp olive oil

1 tsp dijon mustard

2 tsp honey

½ tsp salt

½ ground black pepper

Instructions:

1. Place your salad ingredients in a bowl and toss well.

2. In a small bowl, place your oil, vinegar, mustard and honey. Whisk until well-blended.

3. Pour your dressing over the salad. Season with salt and pepper.

4. Toss thoroughly to ensure an even coating.

5. Serve and enjoy!

Pork and bean soup

🕐 1 hr 30 mins

🐷 6 servings

Ingredients:

1 cup pulled pork

1 can chopped tomatoes

1 can white beans

1 white onion, diced

1.5 cups beef broth

1 cup kale, shredded

3 cloves garlic, minced

3 tbsp tomato paste

1 tbsp smoked paprika

½ tbsp chili powder

1 tbsp brown sugar

½ tsp salt

½ tsp ground black pepper

1 tbsp olive oil

Instructions:

1. Heat your oil in a pan and fry your onions and garlic until soft and golden.

2. Add your pork and tomato paste, fry for 2 - 3 minutes, then remove from heat.

3. Take a large saucepan and pour in your pork, tomatoes and beef broth and stir.

4. Bring to the boil and add your beans and seasonings.

5. Cover and reduce heat to a simmer. Allow to cook for about 40 minutes.

6. Add your kale and cook on high for another 15 - 20 minutes.

7. Serve with bread and garnish with parsley.

Hungarian pork and tomato soup

 2 hrs

 4 - 6 servings

Ingredients:

1 cup pulled pork

1 can chopped tomatoes

2 cups chicken broth

2 red bell peppers, sliced

1 white onion, diced

4 cloves garlic, minced

2 tbsp sweet paprika

1 tsp caraway seeds

1 tsp olive oil

2 bay leaves

½ tsp salt

½ tsp ground black pepper

Instructions:

1. Heat your oil in a pan and fry your onion and garlic until soft and golden.

2. Add your bell peppers and fry until soft.

3. Transfer to a large saucepan and add your pork, tomatoes and stock.

4. Bring to the boil and mix in your seasonings.

5. Once boiled, reduce to a simmer and cover. Allow to cook for 1 hour and 30 minutes.

6. Serve with bread and a dollop of sour cream.

Bbq cobb salad

 30 mins

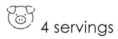 4 servings

Ingredients:

2 cups pulled pork

2 romaine lettuces, shredded

1 avocado, diced

4 hard boiled eggs

1 cup cherry tomatoes, halved

½ cup bbq sauce

Instructions:

- Dice your hard boiled eggs.
- Lay each ingredient out in stripes across your serving platter.
- Drizzle with bbq sauce. I recommend using my recipe from the previous chapter of this book.
- Sprinkle with shredded cheddar or pepper jack cheese (optional).

Creamy comfort food pork soup

 1 hr 30 mins

 6 servings

Ingredients:

1 cup pulled pork

1 cauliflower, chopped

1 carrot, peeled and chopped

1 white onion, diced

4 cloves of garlic, minced

3 cups of chicken broth

1 cup milk

1 tsp paprika

2 tsp oregano

½ tsp salt

1 tsp ground black pepper

1 tbsp olive oil

Instructions:

1. Heat your oil in a pan and fry your onion and garlic until soft and golden.

2. Transfer to a large saucepan and add your cauliflower, carrot, chicken broth and seasonings.

3. Bring to the boil.

4. Once boiling, lower the heat to a simmer and cover.

5. Cook until cauliflower and carrots are soft.

6. Transfer the soup to a blender and add milk. Pulse until smooth.

7. Return soup to the saucepan and add the pork. Simmer for a further 30 minutes.

8. Serve with crusty bread.

Southwest shredded pork salad

 30 mins

 10 servings

Ingredients:

1.5 cups pulled pork

1 whole iceberg lettuce, shredded

2 romaine lettuces, shredded

1 cup black beans

1 red onion, diced

2 tomatoes, diced

1 avocado, diced

For the dressing:

¾ cup mayonnaise

½ cup buttermilk

2 tbsp bbq sauce

2 tbsp apple cider vinegar

1 tsp smoked paprika

1 tsp dill

1 tsp garlic powder

½ tsp salt

½ tsp ground black pepper

Instructions:

1. Mix your dressing ingredients well in a small bowl. For bbq sauce, i recommend using my recipe from the previous chapter of this book.

2. In a large salad bowl, mix your dry ingredients.

3. Pour the dressing over the salad and toss well to ensure even coverage.

4. Sprinkle with a crumbled soft cheese (optional) and serve.

Pulled pork salad Vietnamese style

 30 mins

 4 servings

Ingredients:

1 cup pulled pork

2 cups white cabbage, shredded

1 carrot, julienned

1 cucumber, julienned

3 green onions, chopped

¼ cup cilantro, chopped

¼ cup mint leaves, chopped

For the dressing:

1 lime, juiced

1 tbsp peanut oil

1 tbsp fish sauce

1 tbsp soy sauce

1 tsp sriracha

½ tsp honey

½ clove garlic, minced

Instructions:

1. Toss your salad vegetables well in a large salad bowl.

2. Mix your dressing ingredients well in a small bowl.

3. Empty the dressing over the salad and toss to ensure a thorough coating.

4. Top the vegetables with pork, spreading it out as much as possible.

5. Garnish with crushed peanuts and thinly sliced red chili peppers.

Pork and caramelized onion tartlets

 1 hr 30 mins

 10 servings

Ingredients:

1.5 cups pulled pork

1 sheet puff pastry

2 red onions, thinly sliced

1 egg, beaten.

1 tbsp balsamic vinegar

1 tbsp olive oil

¼ tsp salt

¼ tsp ground black pepper

Instructions:

1. Fry your onions in the olive oil until soft. Add the balsamic vinegar, salt and pepper, and sauteé until brown.

2. Preheat your oven to 400 degrees.

3. Roll out your puff pastry. I recommend using my recipe for puff pastry from the previous chapter of this book.

4. Spread your caramelized onions on the pastry dough. Leave about ½ inch around the borders. Top with pork.

5. Wash the untopped borders with egg.

6. Place on a paper-lined baking tray.

7. Bake in the oven for 10 - 15 minutes or until the pastry is golden and puffed.

8. Cut into 20 slices and serve with crumbled goat cheese (optional).

Maple pulled pork and poached egg

 30 mins

 4 servings

Ingredients:

2 cups pulled pork

4 cups spinach leaves

4 eggs

¼ cup goat cheese, crumbled

1 tbsp apple cider vinegar

For the dressing:

½ cup olive oil

¼ cup apple cider vinegar

2 tbsp maple syrup

1 tsp dijon mustard

½ tsp salt

½ tsp ground black pepper

Instructions:

1. Mix your dressing ingredients in a small bowl and leave to chill, covered, in the fridge.

2. Bring about an inch and a half of water to a simmer in a pan or skillet.

3. Add a tablespoon of vinegar to the water and stir to create a small whirlpool.

4. Break your eggs into a bowl to add into the pan one by one.

5. Tip the eggs, one at a time, into the middle of the whirlpool.

6. Cook for 3-4 minutes or until the outside of the egg has turned completely white and firm.

7. Place one cup of spinach on each plate. Top with pork.

8. Gently place an egg on top of each plate.

9. Sprinkle with your crumbled cheese and drizzle with dressing. Serve.

Pulled pork gyoza

 1 hr

 10 servings

Ingredients:

1 cup pulled pork

1 pack round dumpling wrappers

2 cups cabbage, shredded

2 cloves garlic, minced

1.5 inches ginger, minced

2 green onions, very finely chopped

2 tbsp soy sauce

2 tbsp sesame oil

1 tbsp sweet sake

¼ cup water

Instructions:

1. Heat 1 tbsp of oil in a pan and add the pork, cabbage, garlic, ginger, soy sauce and sake. Fry until

most of the moisture has disappeared and the cabbage has wilted.

2. Remove from heat and allow to cool.

3. Lay out your wrappers on a cool surface. Wet the outer edges of the wraps using a few drops of water on your fingers.

4. Place about 1 tablespoon of your pork and cabbage mixture into the center of each wrap. Sprinkle with green onions.

5. Fold the wrap in half and close by pinching and folding the edges.

6. Heat the remaining sesame oil in a saucepan. Once hot, place your gyoza in the pot with the seams facing up.

7. When the bottoms have browned, pour the water into the pot and cover. Reduce heat to a simmer to allow the gyoza to steam.

8. When the wrappers become translucent, the gyoza are ready.

9. Serve with soy sauce or teriyaki for dipping.

Pork and mushroom vol-au-vents

 1 hr

 4 servings

Ingredients:

1 cup pulled pork

1 sheet puff pastry

2 cups mushrooms of your choice

½ cup cream

1 ½ tbsp melted butter

1 clove garlic, minced

1 egg, beaten

2 tbsp parmesan cheese, finely grated

½ tbsp thyme, dried

½ tbsp cracked black   pepper

½ tsp salt

½ tsp smoked paprika

Instructions:

1. Melt your butter in a pan and add your mushrooms and garlic. Fry until the mushrooms have softened.

2. Add the pork and fry for an additional 3 minutes.

3. Add cream and reduce heat. Simmer, making sure not to bring to the boil.

4. Add thyme, pepper, salt, parmesan and paprika. Stir until thick and remove from heat.

5. Roll out your pastry until ¼ inch thick.

6. Cut into circles and pierce several times with a fork.

7. Place on a paper-lined baking tray and wash with egg.

8. Place into a preheated oven at 390 degrees, and bake for 15 minutes or until pastry is golden brown.

9. Remove from heat and allow to cool on a wire rack for 5 minutes.

10. Gently cut a circle on top of the pastries, and scoop out ⅛ - ¼ of an inch of pastry.

11. Fill the area you've just hollowed with your pork and mushroom mixture.

12. Serve with an additional sprinkling of parmesan cheese (optional).

Pulled pork fritters

 45 mins - 1 hr

 4 servings

Ingredients:

1 cup pulled pork

2 cups mashed potatoes

2 granny smith apples, cored and shredded

2 eggs

3 cloves garlic, minced

1 tbsp cornstarch

1 tbsp dijon mustard

¼ cup chives, chopped

2 tbsp olive oil

Instructions:

1. Mix your potatoes, pork, apples, eggs, garlic, cornstarch, mustard, seasonings and chives in a large bowl.

2. When thoroughly mixed, scoop a handful of the mixture into your hands and form a ball. Repeat until you have used all the mixture.

3. Roughly flatten each ball until it resembles a small pancake, about 1 inch thick.

4. Heat your oil in a frying pan and cook each fritter one at a time.

5. Fry for 3 - 4 minutes on each side or until golden brown.

6. Remove from heat and rest on kitchen paper to remove excess oil.

7. Serve and enjoy!

Spicy pulled pork baked eggs

 1 hr

 4 servings

Ingredients:

1 cup pulled pork

4 eggs

½ cup chorizo, diced

1 can chopped tomatoes

1 white onion, diced

2 cloves garlic, minced

1 orange bell pepper, sliced

2 cups spinach

¼ cup feta cheese, crumbled

1 tbsp olive oil

1 tsp smoked paprika

1 tsp oregano

½ tsp chili flakes

½ tsp salt

½ ground black pepper

Instructions:

1. Heat your oil in a skillet and add the onion and garlic. Fry until soft and golden.

2. Add your chorizo and fry until the meat releases an orange-colored oil.

3. Throw in the pork, spinach and bell pepper and fry until the spinach wilts and pepper softens.

4. Add chopped tomatoes and reduce heat to a simmer. Stir in spices and seasonings.

5. Preheat your oven to 390.

6. Crack the eggs onto your tomato and pork mixture, making sure to keep the yolks intact.

7. Bake in the oven for 15 minutes or until eggs are fully cooked.

8. Sprinkle with feta and serve with crusty bread.

Pork and apple focaccia

 2 hrs

 12 - 15 servings

Ingredients:

2 cups pulled pork

2 ½ cups flour

¼ cup olive oil

1 packet of dry yeast

1 cup warm water

½ cup sharp cheddar, shredded

3 gala apples, cored and thinly sliced

2 cloves garlic, minced

1 tbsp fresh rosemary, roughly torn

1 tsp salt

1 tsp cracked black pepper

Instructions:

1. Combine the yeast with the warm water and allow to sit for 5 minutes or until foamy.

2. Add half of your flour and half your oil and mix well.

3. Sprinkle flour on your workspace and knead the dough, working in the remaining flour.

4. Return the dough to your bowl. Cover and leave for up to 1 hour or until the dough has doubled in size.

5. Preheat your oven to 400 degrees.

6. Oil a baking tray and carefully shape your dough to fill the entire tray.

7. Using your fingers or the bottom of a fork, create dimples in the surface of the dough.

8. Wash the dough with your remaining oil.

9. Sprinkle the garlic, herbs and cheese across the dough.

10. Layer your slices of apple and cover with pork.

11. Leave for about 20 minutes or until the dough has puffed slightly.

12. Bake for 15-20 minutes or until golden brown.

13. Cool on a wire rack for 5 minutes before serving.

Bbq pork dim sum

 2 hrs 30 mins

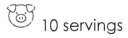 10 servings

Ingredients:

1.5 cups pulled pork

¼ cup shallots, chopped

½ cup chicken broth

½ cup bbq sauce

2 tbsp soy sauce

1 tbsp sesame oil

For the dough:

2 cups flour

1 tbsp dry yeast

½ cup warm water

2 tbsp vegetable oil

1 tbsp sugar

1 tsp baking powder

½ tsp salt

Instructions:

1. Mix your yeast with your warm water and leave for 5 minutes or until foamy.

2. Sift flour into a large bowl and mix with sugar, baking powder, salt and oil.

3. Add your yeast mixture and mix well.

4. Cover bowl and leave for 2 hours or until the dough has more than doubled in size.

5. Heat your sesame oil in a wok and add your shallots. Fry until soft.

6. Add your pork, soy sauce and bbq sauce. I recommend using my bbq sauce recipe from the previous chapter of this book.

7. Stir fry for about 3 - 4 minutes before adding the chicken broth. Bring to a boil.

8. Once your mixture has boiled, reduce to a simmer and cook until the moisture has reduced by two thirds.

9. Knead your dough and separate into ten balls of equal size.

10. On a floured surface, roll the balls out into discs.

11. Fill the discs with your filling and pinch closed.

12. Place each bun onto a square of parchment paper.

13. Bring a cup of water to boil and add to a bamboo steamer.

14. Place your buns in the steamer and allow to cook for 12 - 15 minutes.

Mustard greens and pulled pork

 30 mins

 4 servings

Ingredients:

2 cups pulled pork

3 cups mustard greens, stemmed and washed

1 inch ginger, minced

2 cloves garlic, minced

2.5 tbsp soy sauce

1 tbsp honey

1 tbsp sesame oil

1 small red chili, chopped

½ tsp salt

½ tsp ground black pepper

Garnish: sesame seeds

Instructions:

1. Heat your oil in a wok and add you garlic and ginger. Fry until soft.

2. Add your mustard greens, stir-frying roughly to coat the vegetables in the infused oil.

3. Toss in your pork, soy sauce, honey, chilies and seasonings.

4. Stir fry until your greens have wilted and the pork is sizzling.

5. Serve with a sprinkling of sesame seeds.

Chickpea, pork and chorizo soup

 40 mins

 4 servings

Ingredients:

1 cup pulled pork

½ cup chorizo, diced

1 cup chicken stock

1 can chickpeas

1 can chopped tomatoes

1 red onion, diced

2 cloves garlic, minced

1 cup spinach

2 sticks celery, chopped

1 tbsp olive oil

½ tbsp paprika

1 tsp chili powder

1 tsp cumin

½ tsp salt

½ cracked black pepper

Instructions:

1. Heat your oil in a saucepan and add your garlic and onions. Fry until soft.

2. Add your chorizo and fry until it releases an orange-colored oil.

3. Stir in your pork and pour in the tomatoes and chicken broth.

4. Add the chickpeas, celery, spices and seasonings. Bring to the boil.

5. Once boiled, reduce to a simmer and cover. Allow to cook for 20 minutes.

6. Add the spinach and cook until the leaves have wilted.

7. Serve with fresh, crusty bread.

Cheesy pork pinwheels

 30 mins

10 servings

Ingredients:

1 cup pulled pork

½ cup bbq sauce

2 cups cheddar cheese

1 egg, beaten

1 sheet puff pastry

Instructions:

1. Roll out your pastry into a rectangle on a floured workspace. I recommend using my puff pastry recipe from the previous chapter of this book.

2. Mix your pork and bbq sauce. I recommend using my bbq sauce recipe from the previous chapter of this book.

3. Spread your bbq pork mixture liberally across the pastry dough.

4. Sprinkle the dough with cheese.

5. Roll your pastry tightly, then cut into ten slices of equal size.

6. Preheat your oven to 400 degrees.

7. Line a baking tray with parchment paper, and lay each slice down.

8. Wash each slice with your egg.

9. Bake for 15 - 20 minutes or until golden.

Homemade pork and mushroom ravioli

 1 hr

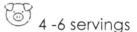 4 -6 servings

Ingredients:

1 cup pulled pork

1 cup mushrooms

1 white onion, diced

2 cloves garlic, minced

¼ cup parmesan cheese

⅛ cup fresh basil, chopped

1 tbsp olive oil

½ tsp salt

½ tsp ground black pepper

For the pasta:

3 cups flour

2 eggs

½ cup water

1 tsp salt

Instructions:

1. Sift your flour into a bowl and add the eggs, water and salt. Mix well.

2. Knead the dough. Cover and leave for 20 minutes.

3. Heat your oil in a frying pan and add your onion, garlic and mushrooms. Fry until soft.

4. Add pork and basil and fry for an additional 2 minutes.

5. Remove from heat and empty into a sieve to remove excess oil and moisture.

6. Empty into a bowl and stir parmesan, salt and pepper.

7. Flour your workspace and roll out your dough until 1/16 inch thick.

8. Cut your dough in half horizontally.

9. On the bottom half, spoon your filling out leaving an inch between each spoonful.

10. Wet the edges of your dough with water and place the top half of the dough over your fillings.

11. Slice the dough into individual, filled squares. Pinch the edges closed with wet fingers.

12. Bring a pot of lightly salted water to the boil.

13. Add your ravioli and cook for 1 - 2 minutes or until your ravioli float to the top.

14. Serve with your choice of sauce or pesto.

Pulled pork spanish omelette

 50 mins

 6 servings

Ingredients:

1 cup pulled pork

1 cup potatoes, peeled and thinly sliced

1 white onion, diced

1 red bell pepper, sliced

5 eggs, beaten

2 tbsp olive oil

1 tsp paprika

1 tsp garlic powder

½ tsp salt

½ tsp ground black pepper

Instructions:

1. Heat your oil in a skillet and add the onions, peppers and potatoes.

2. Reduce the heat and cook for 15 - 20 minutes or until the potatoes are cooked through.

3. Add your pork.

4. Mix your seasonings with your beaten eggs.

5. Add your eggs to the skillet and shape the omelette.

6. Fry for 15 minutes or until the bottom begins to brown.

7. Place skillet under a grill or broiler and cook for an additional 5 - 10 minutes or until the top has become firm and golden.

8. Slice into 6 portions and serve.

ENTREES

Maple pulled pork pizza

2 hrs

8 servings

Ingredients:

1.5 cups pulled pork

Pizza dough

½ cup marinara sauce

½ cup mozzarella cheese

½ cup sharp cheddar cheese

½ red onion, sliced

2 green onions, chopped

1 tbsp maple syrup

1 tbsp apple cider vinegar

½ tsp chili powder

½ tsp garlic powder

Instructions:

1. Preheat your oven to 450 degrees.

2. Roll out your pizza dough on a floured surface. I recommend using my pizza dough recipe from "buffalo pork tear and share bread" in the second chapter of this book.

3. Spoon your marinara sauce onto the dough and spread.

4. Sprinkle your cheeses and red onion.

5. In a bowl, mix the maple syrup, vinegar, chili powder and garlic powder. Add your pork and mix, making sure to liberally coat the meat.

6. Add the meat to the top of your pizza.

7. Put in the oven and allow to bake for 15 - 20 minutes or until the crust is brown.

8. Sprinkle with green onions, cut into 8 slices and enjoy!

Greek-style pulled pork gyros

 30 mins

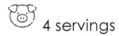 4 servings

Ingredients:

2 cups pulled pork

4 flatbreads or pitas

2 tomatoes, diced

1 red onion, diced

2 romaine lettuces, shredded

For the tzatziki sauce:

1 cup greek yogurt

½ lemon, juiced

½ cucumber, grated

2 tbsp olive oil

1 tbsp fresh dill, chopped

2 cloves garlic, minced

½ tsp salt

Instructions:

1. Using a cheesecloth or kitchen paper, squeeze out as much moisture from the grated cucumber as you can.

2. Add the cucumber to the greek yogurt, and mix in the rest of the tzatziki ingredients. Cover and chill in the fridge until needed.

3. Heat your bread under a broiler/grill or in the microwave. When heating under a broiler, sprinkle with a few drops of water first to prevent from drying out.

4. Load your breads with lettuce, tomato and onion and then top with liberal amounts of pork.

5. Spoon the tzatziki on top of your pork, fold and enjoy!

6. Serve with a greek salad or fries.

Smoky pulled pork hash

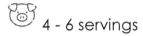 40 mins

4 - 6 servings

Ingredients:

2 cups pulled pork

2 cups russet potatoes, peeled and diced

1 cup cheddar cheese

½ cup bbq sauce

1 white onion, diced

1 orange bell pepper, diced

3 green onions, chopped

½ cup cherry tomatoes, halved

4 eggs

2 cloves garlic, minced

2 tbsp melted butter

1 tsp smoked paprika

½ tsp salt

½ tsp ground black pepper

Instructions:

1. Bring a pot of water to boil and parboil your potatoes for 5 - 10 minutes or until you can pierce them with a fork with little resistance.

2. In a skillet, fry your onions and garlic in the melted butter. Fry until soft and golden.

3. When your potatoes are parboiled, drain well and add to the skillet. Fry until they start to become crisp outside.

4. Add the pepper and tomatoes.

5. Mix your pork with the bbq sauce. I recommend using my bbq sauce recipe from the second chapter of this book.

6. Add your pork and seasonings to the skillet and fry for an additional 10 - 15 minutes.

7. Crack your eggs carefully into the skillet, taking care to keep the yolks intact.

8. Sprinkle with cheese and place the skillet under a broiler/grill.

9. Cook for 15 minutes or until the eggs are fully cooked.

10. Sprinkle with green onions and serve with crusty bread.

Mexican pulled pork tacos

 20 mins

6 - 8 servings

Ingredients:

3 cups pulled pork

1 pack soft tortillas

2 cups romaine lettuce, shredded

2 cups salsa

1 cup pepper jack cheese, shredded

1 cup sour cream

2 avocados, diced

½ cup jalapenos, sliced

1 tbsp olive oil

1 clove garlic, minced

1 tsp cumin

1 tsp paprika

½ tsp salt

½ ground black pepper

½ lime, juiced

Instructions:

1. Heat your oil in a frying pan and add your garlic. Fry until soft and golden.

2. Add your pork, spices, seasonings and lime juice. Fry roughly for 5 minutes, ensuring the meat is thoroughly seasoned.

3. Heat your tortillas under a broiler/grill or in the microwave. If heating under a broiler, sprinkle with a few drops of water first to avoid drying the tortilla.

4. Layer your lettuce, avocado and pork in the tortillas.

5. Top with cheese and salsa. I recommend using my salsa recipe from the second chapter of this book.

6. Top with sour cream and jalapenos to taste.

7. Fold and eat!

Korean pulled pork bibimbap

 1 hr

 6 servings

Ingredients:

2 cups pulled pork

6 cups spinach

1 large carrot, peeled into thin strips

2 cups shiitake mushrooms, sliced

6 eggs

3 cups white rice

1 zucchini, julienned

3 cloves garlic, minced

2 inches ginger, minced

3 tbsp sesame oil

2 tbsp rice vinegar

2 tbsp soy sauce

2 tbsp toasted sesame seeds

1 tbsp dried chili flakes

1 tsp honey

½ tsp salt

½ tsp ground black pepper

Instructions:

1. Boil your rice in a pot using two cups of water for each cup of rice.

2. Place your thin slices of carrot in a bowl with your rice vinegar, salt and honey. Put to one side.

3. Heat one tablespoon of oil in a frying pan or wok and add one clove of garlic. Fry until soft and golden.

4. Add your mushrooms and one tablespoon of soy sauce. Fry until mushrooms are soft. Drain any excess fluid and continue to fry until mushrooms brown slightly.

5. In a clean pan or wok, heat one tablespoon of oil and add one clove garlic and ginger. Fry until soft.

6. Add your zucchini and fry until soft.

7. Heat your remaining oil in a frying pan or wok and add your remaining garlic. Fry until soft.

8. Add your spinach and fry until wilted.

9. Pour your remaining soy sauce over the spinach and fry for an additional 1 - 2 minutes.

10. Poach your eggs in a pot or skillet of simmering water. For tips on how to poach eggs, check out my maple pulled pork and poached egg recipe from the previous chapter.

11. Fill six bowls with your rice. Sprinkle lightly with chili flakes.

12. Spoon your pork and vegetables onto the rice.

13. Top each bowl with a poached egg.

14. Garnish with additional chili flakes and sesame seeds.

Pulled pork perogies

 1 hr 30 mins

6 servings

Ingredients:

1 cup pulled pork

½ white onion, diced

¼ cup bbq sauce

2 tbsp olive oil

For the dough:

2 cups flour

1 egg

½ cup warm water

¼ cup sour cream

1 tsp salt

Instructions:

1. In a large bowl, mix your egg, warm water, sour cream and salt.

2. Gradually sift your flour into the mixture, stirring constantly, until a thick dough forms.

3. Cover the dough and allow to sit for up to an hour.

4. Heat one tablespoon of oil in a frying pan and add your onion. Fry until soft and golden.

5. Add your pork and bbq sauce. I recommend using my bbq sauce recipe from the second chapter of this book.

6. Remove from heat and allow to cool.

7. On a floured surface, roll out your dough until 1/32 inch thick. Basically, as thin as it can get without tearing.

8. Cut the dough into circles.

9. Fill each circle with your bbq pork. Using wet fingertips, fold the dough and pinch closed.

10. Heat your oil in a frying pan. Fry each pierogi until golden and crisp.

11. Serve with your choice of sides.

Cinnamon-spiced pulled pork chili

 2+ hrs

6 - 8 servings

Ingredients:

2 cups pulled pork

1 white onion, diced

2 cloves garlic, minced

1 can chopped tomatoes

1 1/2 cup water

1 can red kidney beans

½ cup sweet corn

1 tbsp olive oil

1 tbsp paprika

½ tbsp cinnamon

2 tsp chili powder

1 tsp cayenne powder

1 tsp garlic powder

½ tsp salt

½ tsp ground black pepper

Instructions:

1. In a pot or large saucepan heat your oil. Add your onion and garlic, and fry until soft and golden.

2. Add your pork and cinnamon. Fry for 1 minute.

3. Pour in the tomatoes, one cup of water, beans and corn. Lower the heat to a simmer.

4. Add in your spices and seasonings and stir well.

5. Cover the pot and allow to simmer for an hour.

6. Stir after an hour and add half a cup of water. Allow to simmer for another 30 minutes.

7. The longer you simmer, the more chance the flavors have to infuse. You can choose to serve after an hour and a half or leave for longer.

8. Serve with rice or tortilla chips, and top with your choice of cheese or sour cream.

Pulled pork buddha bowl

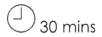 30 mins

 4 servings

Ingredients:

2 cups pulled pork

1 cup quinoa, dry

1 cup salsa

1 cup black-eyed beans

2 avocados, diced

2 cloves garlic, minced

½ white onion, diced

1 tbsp olive oil

½ lime, juiced

1 tsp cumin

½ tsp salt

½ tsp ground black pepper

Instructions:

1. Place your quinoa in a pot with two cups of water. Bring to a boil, then reduce to a simmer and cover. Cook until all the water is absorbed.

2. Heat your oil in a frying pan and add your onion and garlic. Fry until soft and golden.

3. Add your beans, and mix in your spices and seasonings.

4. Separate the quinoa into four bowls.

5. Top each bowl with equal amounts of pork, beans, avocado and salsa. I recommend using my salsa recipe from the second chapter of this book.

6. Optionally top the bowls with sour cream and/or cheese and enjoy!

Pulled pork sloppy joes

 30 mins

4 servings

Ingredients:

2 cups pulled pork

4 brioche buns

1 can chopped tomatoes

½ cup ketchup

2 tbsp apple cider vinegar

1 tbsp brown sugar

1 tsp garlic powder

1 tsp tabasco

½ tsp salt

½ tsp pepper

Instructions:

1. For the brioche buns you can either buy them ready-made or try my recipe from "bbq pulled pork sliders" in the second chapter of this book.

2. In a saucepan combine your pork with your wet ingredients, spices and seasonings. Cover and simmer until thick. If the mixture has a lot of fluid, continue to simmer until it has reached the desired consistency.

3. Cut your brioche buns in half and messily fill with your sloppy joe pork mixture.

4. Serve with coleslaw, fries and/or the side of your choice.

Pulled pork burrito

 1 hr

 6 servings

Ingredients:

2 cups pulled pork

1 cup rice

2 cups chicken broth

6 flour tortillas

1 cup black or pinto beans

1 cup salsa

½ cup sour cream

½ cup cheddar cheese, shredded

½ cup cilantro, chopped

½ lime, juiced

Instructions:

1. Combine your rice and chicken broth in a pot and bring to the boil.

2. Heat your tortillas under a broiler or in the microwave so they are pliable.

3. When all the moisture has been absorbed by the rice, add the cilantro and lime juice. Mix well.

4. On a heated tortilla, spoon out a line of rice.

5. Top with beans, pork and salsa. I recommend using my salsa recipe from the second chapter of this book.

6. Next top with sour cream and/or cheese to your taste.

7. For an added kick, you can add slices of pickled jalapenos before wrapping your burrito.

8. Wrap tightly and enjoy!

Banh mi

 30 mins

 4 servings

Ingredients:

2 cups pulled pork

2 large baguettes

1 carrot, grated

1 daikon radish, grated

1 cucumber, sliced

½ white cabbage, shredded

½ cup mayonnaise

2 tbsp rice vinegar

1 tbsp brown sugar

¼ cup cilantro, chopped

1 red chili, thinly sliced

Instructions:

1. In a bowl mix your vinegar, sugar and vegetables. Put to one side.

2. Toast your baguettes and cut in half. Cut across horizontally to allow for filling.

3. Liberally spread mayonnaise in your baguettes.

4. Top with pork, then add your pickled vegetables.

5. Sprinkle with cilantro and red chilis.

6. Serve and enjoy!

Pork and bean stew

 2 hrs

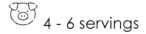 4 - 6 servings

Ingredients:

2 cups pulled pork

½ cup black beans

½ cup black-eyed beans

1 white onion, chopped

2 cloves garlic, minced

1 carrot, peeled and diced

2 large potatoes, peeled and diced

2 cups beef broth

2 tsp oregano

2 tsp rosemary

1 tbsp olive oil

½ tsp salt

½ tsp ground black pepper

Instructions:

1. Heat your oil in a large saucepan and add your onions and garlic. Fry until soft and golden.

2. Add your pork, beans, potato, carrot and ¾ of your beef broth.

3. Bring to a boil and reduce to a simmer.

4. Add your herbs and seasonings. Cover and cook for 1 hour.

5. After an hour, add your remaining stock and once again cover and cook.

6. When the moisture has reduced by half, serve.

Fettuccine with pork ragu

 1 hr

 6 servings

Ingredients:

2 cups pulled pork

1 can chopped tomatoes

½ cup red wine

½ cup chicken broth

2 tbsp tomato paste

4 cloves garlic, minced

1 white onion, diced

1 cup basil, chopped

2 tbsp oregano

1 tbsp olive oil

1 tsp salt

1 tsp ground black pepper

1 pound fresh egg fettuccine or make your own

Instructions:

1. In a large saucepan, heat your oil and fry the onions and garlic until soft and golden.

2. Add pork, tomatoes, broth, wine and herbs. Bring to a boil.

3. Reduce to a simmer, cover and cook.

4. Allow to cook for 30 minutes or until moisture has reduced by a third.

5. Fill another pot with lightly salted water and bring to the boil.

6. You can use store-bought pasta or try my pasta dough recipe from the previous chapter.

7. Once the water is boiled, add your pasta. Cook for 2 minutes or until the pasta floats to the top.

8. Drain the pasta well.

9. Dish up pasta in bowls and top with the pork ragu.

10. Sprinkle with additional chopped basil and/or parmesan cheese.

Pulled pork pot pie

 1 hr

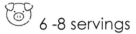 6 -8 servings

Ingredients:

2 cups pulled pork

2 cups mushrooms, sliced

1 white onion, diced

2 cloves garlic, minced

1 carrot, peeled and diced

3 potatoes, peeled and diced

1 cup chicken broth

1 cup cream

1 tbsp olive oil

1 egg, beaten

2 tsp smoked paprika

1 tsp salt

1 tsp ground black pepper

Pie crust

Instructions:

1. Preheat your oven to 400 degrees.

2. Heat your oil in a pan and fry your garlic and onions until soft and golden.

3. Separate your pie crust into two balls, and roll one ball out on a floured work surface. You can use store-bought pastry or use my shortcrust pastry recipe from my mini quiche recipe in the second chapter of this book.

4. Roll with a rolling pin until ¼ inch thick.

5. Lay the pastry gently into a greased casserole dish, pie dish or dutch oven. Make sure it covers the bottom and the sides without tearing.

6. Add your garlic and onions into a bowl along with the pork, vegetables, broth, cream, spices and seasonings. Mix well.

7. Gently empty the bowl into the pie dish.

8. Roll the remaining dough with a rolling pin until ¼ inch thick.

9. Carefully lay your pastry over the dish.

10. Pierce with a fork across the pastry.

11. Wash the surface of the dough with your beaten egg.

12. Bake for 30 - 40 minutes or until pastry is golden brown.

13. Slice and serve.

Tonkotsu ramen with pulled pork

 2+ hrs

 6 servings

Ingredients:

2 cups pulled pork

2 cups cooked ramen noodles

6 hard boiled eggs

2 cups shiitake mushrooms

½ cup dried seaweed

3 green onions, sliced

1 tbsp sesame oil

For the broth:

1 pork bone

1 cup chicken bones

2 pigs trotters, chopped

1 full bulb of garlic, roughly chopped

1 large white onion, unpeeled and halved

1 leek, chopped

2 inches ginger, sliced

½ cup white oyster mushrooms

Instructions:

1. The most important part of this dish is the broth. It can take up to 12 hours to make, so make sure to give yourself plenty of time.

2. Place your trotters, pork bone (make sure to get a picnic shoulder or boston butt with bone in) and chicken bones in a pot filled with water. Bring to the boil.

3. When boiled, remove from the heat immediately and drain.

4. Wash off any dark marrow or blood from the bones and return to the empty pot.

5. Heat your sesame oil in a pan and fry your garlic, onion and ginger for 1 minute before adding to your bones and trotters.

6. Add your mushrooms and leeks, fill the pot with water and bring to a boil.

7. Once boiled, reduce to a simmer and cover with a lid. Remove any scum or grease that floats to the top with a spoon.

8. Cook for 6 - 10 hours or until the broth is thick and creamy in appearance.

9. Spoon the broth into bowls and add cooked ramen, shredded pork, halved hard boiled eggs and shiitake mushrooms.

10. Garnish with sprinkled green onions and thin sheets of seaweed.

Pulled pork mac 'n' cheese

 45 mins

 6 servings

Ingredients:

2 cups pulled pork

3 cups pasta

4 cups milk

1 cup cheddar cheese, shredded

½ cup mozzarella cheese, shredded

½ cup swiss cheese, shredded

¼ cup flour

¼ cup butter

½ tbsp dijon mustard

½ tsp salt

½ tsp ground black pepper

Bbq sauce (optional)

Instructions:

1. Boil your pasta in a large pot. Once cooked, drain and put to one side.

2. In a saucepan melt your butter and gradually add your flour, stirring constantly.

3. Gradually add your milk, still stirring, adding more only when the mixture is smooth.

4. Empty in your cheese and mustard and simmer. Be sure to leave half of your cheddar for later.

5. Stir in your salt, pepper and pork. Stir until the pork is thoroughly coated in the cheese sauce.

6. Preheat your oven to 350 degrees.

7. Grease a casserole dish with butter and pour in your pasta.

8. Pour your sauce over the pasta and stir well.

9. Sprinkle with the remaining cheddar cheese and place in the oven.

10. Bake for 20 - 30 minutes or until cheese is bubbling and golden brown.

11. Drizzle with bbq sauce (optional) and enjoy!

Pulled pork and sesame zoodles

 30 mins

 4 servings

Ingredients:

2 cups pulled pork

4 zucchinis, spiralized

1 cup sugar snap peas

1 cup broccolini

1 red bell pepper, sliced

2 cloves garlic, minced

1 inch ginger, minced

1 tbsp tahini

1 tbsp soy sauce

1 tbsp toasted sesame seeds

1 tbsp sesame oil

1 tsp honey

½ tsp salt

½ tsp pepper

Instructions:

1. Heat your oil in a wok and add your garlic and ginger. Fry until soft and golden.

2. Add your broccolini, sugar snap peas, soy sauce, tahini, honey and seasonings. Fry until the broccolini begins to soften.

3. Add the zoodles, pepper, pork and honey. Stir fry until the zoodles are soft but firm.

4. Serve into bowls and garnish with sprinkled sesame seeds.

Pulled pork risotto

 1 hr

 4 servings

Ingredients:

1 cup pulled pork

2 cups arborio rice

4 cups chicken broth

1 cup white wine

1 cup mushrooms, sliced

1 white onion, finely chopped

2 cloves garlic, minced

½ cup parmesan cheese, finely grated

¼ cup butter

½ tsp salt

½ tsp ground black pepper

Instructions:

1. Leave your broth simmering in a pot.

2. Melt your butter in a saucepan and fry your garlic and onions until soft and golden.

3. Add rice and pork.

4. Add enough stock to cover all the ingredients. Add wine and seasonings, cover and simmer.

5. As the stock reduces in volume, add one ladle of stock and stir. Cover, simmer and repeat.

6. On your last ladle of stock, add in your mushrooms.

7. When the last of the moisture has been absorbed by the rice, stir in your cheese.

8. Serve with roasted vegetables or a side salad.

Pulled pork lasagna

 1 hr 20 mins

 6 servings

Ingredients:

3 cups pulled pork

1 pack lasagna sheets

1 can chopped tomatoes

¼ cup red wine

3 cloves garlic, minced

1 white onion, diced

1 tbsp tomato paste

½ cup fresh basil, chopped

1 cup fresh mozzarella, sliced

1 cup ricotta

1 cup parmesan, shredded

1 tbsp olive oil

Instructions:

1. Heat your oil in a pot and add your onions and garlic. Fry until soft and golden.

2. Add pork, tomatoes, tomato paste, wine and basil. Leave to simmer, stirring occasionally.

3. Preheat your oven to 350 degrees.

4. In a greased casserole dish, add a quarter of your meat sauce.

5. Top with pasta sheets. Spread a quarter of your ricotta across the pasta.

6. Top with mozzarella and parmesan.

7. Repeat these steps until the lasagna is fully layered, leaving a layer of mozzarella and parmesan on top.

8. Place in the oven and bake for 30 minutes or until the cheese is bubbling and golden.

9. Cut into 6 slices and serve with the sides of your choice.

Creamy pork carbonara

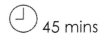 45 mins

 4 servings

Ingredients:

1.5 cups pulled pork

1 lb spaghetti

2 eggs

½ cup parmesan

2 cloves garlic, minced

1 tbsp butter

1 tsp salt

½ tsp ground black pepper

Instructions:

1. Bring a pot of lightly salted water to the boil. Add your spaghetti and cook for 10 minutes or until soft.

2. Heat your butter in a pan and fry your garlic until soft and golden.

3. Beat your eggs and add your cheese, salt and pepper. Mix well.

4. Add your pork to your garlic and reduce heat.

5. When your spaghetti is cooked, drain well and add to the pork and garlic.

6. Pour your egg and cheese mix over the pasta. Mix quickly, ensuring you cover the spaghetti well and prevent the eggs from scrambling.

7. Serve with an extra sprinkling of parmesan cheese or freshly ground pepper.

Printed in Great Britain
by Amazon